NBA's TOP 10
COACHES

BY WILL GRAVES

SportsZone

An Imprint of Abdo Publishing
abdopublishing.com

→ NBA's
TOP 10

10 9 8 7 6 5 4 3 2 1

abdopublishing.com

Published by Abdo Publishing, a division of ABDO, PO Box 398166, Minneapolis, Minnesota 55439. Copyright © 2019 by Abdo Consulting Group, Inc. International copyrights reserved in all countries. No part of this book may be reproduced in any form without written permission from the publisher. SportsZone™ is a trademark and logo of Abdo Publishing.

Printed in the United States of America, North Mankato, Minnesota
042018
092018

**THIS BOOK CONTAINS
RECYCLED MATERIALS**

Cover Photo: Eric Gay/AP Images
Interior Photos: Mike Conroy/AP Images, 4–5; Tony Dejak/AP Images, 6–7; Ron Cortes/KRT/Newscom, 9; CEM/AP Images, 10; Bettmann/Getty Images, 11; AP Images, 13, 23; Mike Kullen/AP Images, 15; John Biever/Sports Illustrated/Getty Images, 16; H. Joe Hooloway Jr./AP Images, 17; David Zalubowski/AP Images, 18–19; Bob Jordan/AP Images, 20; Jerry Wachter/Sports Illustrated/Getty Images, 21; Tony Gutierrez/AP Images, 24–25; The Sporting News/Getty Images, 26; Jeff Haynes/AFP/Getty Images, 27

Editor: Bradley Cole
Series Designer: Craig Hinton

Library of Congress Control Number: 2017962572

Publisher's Cataloging-in-Publication Data

Names: Graves, Will, author.
Title: NBA's top 10 coaches / by Will Graves
Other titles: NBA's top ten coaches
Description: Minneapolis, Minnesota : Abdo Publishing, 2019. | Series: NBA's top 10 |Includes online resources and index.
Identifiers: ISBN 9781532114489 (lib.bdg.) | ISBN 9781532154317 (ebook)
Subjects: LCSH: Basketball coaches--United States--Juvenile literature. | Basketball--Records--United States--Juvenile literature. | Basketball--History--Juvenile literature. | National Basketball Association--Juvenile literature.
Classification: DDC 796.323--dc23

TABLE OF
CONTENTS

INTRODUCTION

Basketball's first coach was a gym teacher. James Naismith was working at a school in Springfield, Massachusetts, in 1891. Naismith was looking for something to do indoors that could keep his students busy. And basketball was born.

Naismith came up with the original 13 rules for the game. He spent the rest of his life helping others learn the sport as interest grew. More than 125 years later, the game has spread across the globe. But a coach's goals remain the same. They try to help their players improve while also helping them learn to play as a team.

Some coaches taught lessons better than anyone else in National Basketball Association (NBA) history. Some, like Red Auerbach, were larger-than-life personalities. Others preferred to let their players do the talking, like Lenny Wilkens. No matter how they went about their job, they all found a way to get the best out of their teams.

10

Steve Kerr has quickly become one of the NBA's top coaches. →

STEVE KERR

Steve Kerr didn't have any coaching experience when the Golden State Warriors hired him in May 2014. Kerr did, however, know a thing or two about what it takes to win. He spent 15 years as one of the best three-point shooters in the NBA. Along the way, he was a part of two of the greatest dynasties in modern NBA history. Kerr won three championships with Michael Jordan and the Chicago Bulls from 1996–98 and earned two more rings with Tim Duncan and the San Antonio Spurs.

Kerr retired in 2003 as the most accurate three-point shooter in NBA history. Kerr spent time as a television analyst and as general manager for the Phoenix Suns before interviewing with Golden State. Kerr had a plan when he went into his job interview. He put together a video titled "Why I'm Ready To Be A Head Coach." Turns out, Kerr was right. In 2014 he took over a Warriors team that kept falling short in the playoffs even though it had budding stars Stephen Curry and Klay Thompson on the roster. He wasted little time winning over Curry and the rest of the Warriors. Kerr encouraged his players to share the ball, play defense, and let the three-pointers fly.

The Warriors went 67–15 in Kerr's first season. No rookie coach had ever won more games in NBA history. He also

helped Curry develop into a two-time NBA Most Valuable Player (MVP). Golden State beat the Cleveland Cavaliers in the NBA Finals in 2015 and 2017. Kerr missed much of the 2015–16 season while recovering from back surgery, but the Warriors still won an NBA-record 73 games.

09

LARRY BROWN

Some successful coaches stay with one team for decades. It was that way for Larry Brown's mentor, college legend Dean Smith. Smith coached at the University of North Carolina from 1961, when Brown was a junior guard, until he retired in 1997.

Brown took a very different career path. Brown coached for 11 different professional teams during his long career. That doesn't even include three different college coaching stops, including one at the University of Kansas that netted the Jayhawks a national championship in 1988.

Brown never stayed in one job longer than five years. But no matter where he went, he won. During his 31 seasons on the bench in the American Basketball Association (ABA) and NBA, he won 1,327 games and reached the playoffs 21 times. Brown preached how important it was to "play the right way." For his players, that meant to share the ball, try hard every game, and be a good teammate.

At nearly every stop during his coaching journey, Brown's players embraced his message. His greatest success came late in his career. In 2001 he guided the Philadelphia 76ers and star guard Allen Iverson to the NBA Finals, where they lost to the mighty Los Angeles Lakers.

COACHING TREE

Larry Brown had a knack for finding bright basketball minds to serve as his assistants. Brown's coaching tree extends far and wide. His former assistants include San Antonio Spurs coach Gregg Popovich and standout college coaches John Calipari and Bill Self. Like Brown, Self won a national title at Kansas. He led the Jayhawks to the championship in 2008.

Larry Brown had success everywhere he coached.

Brown gained his revenge three years later, this time coaching the Detroit Pistons. The Pistons played ferocious defense to reach the Finals against Los Angeles. Detroit shut down the Lakers, never allowing more than 99 points in any game, to give Brown his first title.

08

John Kundla celebrated five NBA championships with the Lakers.

JOHN KUNDLA

The NBA wasn't even known as the NBA when John Kundla was named head coach of the Minneapolis Lakers in 1947. The Lakers played in the National Basketball League and had just moved from Detroit to the biggest city in Minnesota. When they moved, they asked Kundla if he would be interested in a new job.

Kundla was just 31 years old at the time and coaching at a small college. The Lakers didn't offer him much money. Kundla made just $6,000 during his first season. His new position did come with a few perks, though.

The Lakers put together an entirely new roster after coming over from Detroit. The group included future Hall of Fame center George Mikan and high-flying forward Jim Pollard. Mikan and Pollard were two of pro basketball's first true superstars.

Though Kundla was usually calm on the sideline, he knew how to send a message to his players. If Mikan made a mistake, Kundla made sure to point it out to the rest of the team. It was Kundla's way of making sure everyone on the

PROFESSIONAL TO AMATEUR

While a lot of coaches use college jobs as a stepping stone to the NBA, John Kundla went the other way. After leaving the Lakers, he coached at his alma mater, the University of Minnesota, from 1959 to 1968, posting a record of 110–105.

Kundla turned the Minneapolis Lakers into one of the first basketball dynasties.

Lakers understood that no player was perfect. Even the best players in the world made mistakes.

Over the next decade, Kundla built the Lakers into one of pro basketball's first dynasties. The league changed names from the National Basketball League to the Basketball Association of America to the NBA, and the Lakers kept right on winning.

Minneapolis won five titles in six years between 1948 and 1954. Kundla stepped down in 1959 with a career record of 423–302 when the owners decided to move the Lakers to Los Angeles.

07

Lenny Wilkens both played for and coached the Seattle SuperSonics.

LENNY WILKENS

The career of one of the best players and coaches in NBA history nearly ended before it even began. Lenny Wilkens barely made his high school team as a freshman and didn't even try out the next two years. Wilkens thought he wasn't good enough to play. He couldn't have been more wrong.

Wilkens made the team as a senior and played well enough to earn a scholarship to Providence College. Wilkens reached the NBA in 1961 with the St. Louis Hawks. By his third season, he was an All-Star.

When he was playing for the Seattle SuperSonics in 1969, the head coaching job came open. Seattle general manager Dick Vertlieb asked Wilkens if he thought he could play and coach at the same time. Wilkens said no at first but changed his mind. He was practically a coach on the floor when he played. He decided he might as well have the actual title.

Wilkens served in both roles until he retired as a player in 1975. Finally able to focus just on coaching, Wilkens's career took off. In 1978 he led the SuperSonics to the NBA Finals, where they lost to the Washington Bullets. A year later, Seattle won a Finals rematch in five games. Wilkens retired in 2005 with 1,332 victories, the most by any coach in NBA history at the time. Fittingly, he is one of the few people to be elected to the Basketball Hall of Fame as both a player and a coach.

TEAM USA

Wilkens coached the 1996 US Olympic team to a gold medal. The 1996 Olympics were only the second Games to allow NBA players to participate and included many members of the 1992 "Dream Team." The 1996 Olympics were in Atlanta, Georgia, where at the time Wilkens was coaching the Atlanta Hawks.

Don Nelson was a fiery presence on the sidelines in his 31 years as an NBA coach.

DON NELSON

Don Nelson was looking for a job in the summer of 1965. That's when the Boston Celtics called and asked the smooth-shooting forward if he wanted to play for one of the NBA's best teams. Legendary Celtics coach Red Auerbach told Nelson he had better be ready to play fast. Even though Boston had one of the best centers ever in Bill Russell, Auerbach made sure the Celtics practiced the fast break regularly.

Nelson fit in perfectly as the Celtics rolled to NBA title after NBA title in the late 1960s and mid-1970s. He retired in 1976 and was offered the head coaching job with the Milwaukee Bucks in 1978. Nelson didn't think he was ready. He told his players during his first practice that he didn't know what he was doing.

Nelson borrowed heavily from the lessons Auerbach taught him, while also adding a few tricks of his own. While some coaches built their teams around good big men, Nelson liked having smaller, quicker players who could get up and down the court in a flash. His preferred style became known across the NBA as "Nellie Ball." Nellie Ball was exciting. While other teams lumbered down the court and waited for their big men to get set up, Nelson's teams almost always just took off running.

Nelson's teams won 50 or more games a season 13 times during his 31 seasons on the sideline. Though he never reached the NBA Finals as a coach, he pulled off one of the most remarkable upsets in playoff history.

In 2007 Nelson guided the eighth-seeded Golden State Warriors past the top-seeded Dallas Mavericks in the first round of the Western Conference playoffs. He retired in 2010 with 1,335 wins, the most of any coach in NBA history. He also won the NBA's Coach of the Year Award three times, tied for the most ever.

05

Chuck Daly coached the Detroit Pistons to two NBA championships.

CHUCK DALY

Chuck Daly ran his teams like a business. He managed the players so that clashing egos wouldn't disrupt the team. He looked the part of a businessman, too, always sporting crisp suits and perfectly coiffed hair.

Daly's coaching career got off to a slow start. He spent eight years coaching at a high school in Punxsutawney, Pennsylvania, before gradually working his way up. He had coaching stops at Boston College and the University of Pennsylvania. He didn't get his first NBA coaching job until 1981, when he went 9–32 for the Cleveland Cavaliers.

A second chance arrived with the Detroit Pistons in 1983. Daly didn't let it go to waste. Daly got Isiah Thomas, Bill Laimbeer, and Dennis Rodman to play together. The Pistons became known for their hard-nosed defense and earned the nickname "Bad Boys" because of their rugged style of play. They went up against Michael Jordan and the Chicago Bulls every year that Jordan was with Chicago. They invented the "Jordan Rules" when playing their rival Bulls.

DREAM TEAM

Chuck Daly won a gold medal while coaching the "Dream Team" during the 1992 Summer Olympics in Barcelona, Spain. With a roster that featured Michael Jordan, Larry Bird, and Magic Johnson, the Americans won their eight games in the tournament by an average of 43.8 points.

Daly was selected as the coach for Team USA and the 1992 Dream Team.

They played with extra aggression every time Jordan got the ball. The Pistons knocked the Bulls out of the playoffs three years in a row on their way to two championships.

Daly left Detroit after the 1992 season and spent time in New Jersey and Orlando, but never quite got back to the top. However, his 1980s run with Detroit's Bad Boys will go down in history as one of the greatest.

04

Gregg Popovich turned the San Antonio Spurs into a consistent NBA title contender.

GREGG POPOVICH

G regg Popovich took an unusual path to the NBA. He played basketball at the Air Force Academy in the 1970s. After graduating, he started working at an Air Force base in California. During his days in the US Air Force, Popovich learned to live by the motto "we shall either find a way or make one." As a basketball coach, Popovich did both.

Popovich slowly made his way up the basketball ranks. He started by coaching high school players at the Air Force preparatory academy, then moved on to Pomona College in California. A one-year detour as a volunteer assistant for Larry Brown at the University of Kansas in 1986–87 changed the course of Popovich's life. Brown was so impressed by Popovich's mind for the game that he brought Popovich along when Brown was named the San Antonio Spurs' head coach in 1988.

Popovich took over the Spurs' head coaching job early in the 1996–97 season. When San Antonio landed the top pick in the NBA Draft the following spring, it chose Wake Forest forward Tim Duncan. Popovich focused on finding a way to make sure Duncan and center David Robinson could work together. The plan worked brilliantly.

The Spurs won their first NBA title in 1999, starting a string of consistency nearly unmatched in the modern NBA. Even as the players around Popovich and Duncan changed, the results did not. San Antonio cut down the nets as champions four more times by the end of the 2013–14 season.

By the 2017–18 season, San Antonio had made the playoffs 20 straight years, winning 70 percent of its games with Popovich in charge. In 2016, he passed his mentor Brown on the NBA's all-time coaching wins list.

03

Pat Riley had success with every NBA team he coached.

PAT RILEY

The Los Angeles Lakers were a bit of a mess in the fall of 1981. Star point guard Earvin "Magic" Johnson had led them to the NBA title during his rookie season in 1979–80. But barely a year later, Johnson was clashing with head coach Paul Westhead and wanted out. Lakers ownership wanted to bring former Lakers star Jerry West back as their new coach. But West insisted that he only would return as an assistant to Pat Riley.

Even though Riley had never been a head coach in the NBA, he knew all about the game. He was a star at the University of Kentucky in the 1960s and played nearly a decade in the NBA. After a stint in the television booth, Riley became a first-year assistant on the Lakers' 1980 championship team. Riley inherited a roster filled with stars, including future Hall of Famers in

With stints at both the New York Knicks and Miami Heat, Pat Riley had several coaching stops in the NBA.

Johnson and center Kareem Abdul-Jabbar. Riley's biggest obstacle was trying to get everyone to play together.

"He knows that if we don't play as a unit, all the talent that we have, we can't win," Johnson said. While Riley wanted his team to focus on defense, he also gave Johnson the freedom to be creative with the offense. And the "Showtime" Lakers were born.

Los Angeles won with style, and Riley fit the role of leading man with his finely tailored suits and slicked-back hair. The Lakers won four championships in nine years with Riley at the helm. He later took the New York Knicks to the NBA Finals in 1994 and built the Miami Heat into a powerhouse, coaching them to their first title in 2006. Riley won the NBA Coach of the Year Award three times, once each with the Lakers, Heat, and Knicks.

Riley moved to the Miami front office in 2008 and put together a roster that won two more titles with stars LeBron James and Dwyane Wade.

02

Bill Russell (6) and Red Auerbach were key figures in the Boston Celtics dynasty.

ARNOLD "RED" AUERBACH

There were plenty of good nights for Arnold "Red" Auerbach during his long career in basketball. But his early days in Boston were just okay. The Celtics were competitive but always had trouble in the playoffs. That changed in 1956 when they traded for rookie center Bill Russell.

Auerbach teamed Russell with flashy point guard Bob Cousy, and the Celtics took off. Boston won the NBA title nine times in Auerbach's final 10 seasons as coach, including eight straight between 1959 and 1966, a record that will likely never be broken. He won 938 games over 20 seasons, 16 of them in Boston.

When Auerbach gave up coaching to focus on organizational duties in 1966, he named Russell to replace him. That made Russell the first black coach in NBA history. Russell won two titles as a player-coach before retiring in 1969.

Auerbach's basketball smarts continued to help the Celtics even after he stepped away from the bench and took a job as the team's general manager. He had a knack for figuring out which players worked well together, helping put the pieces in place for 16 championship teams in all.

RED TO THE RAFTERS

Red Auerbach never played in the NBA. Still, his "number" is retired. The Celtics added No. 2 to their banner of retired numbers on January 4, 1985. The number indicates that the team considers Auerbach the second-most important person in franchise history after team founder Walter Brown.

01

Phil Jackson coached the Los Angeles Lakers to multiple championships.

PHIL JACKSON

Phil Jackson grew up far from the bright lights of professional basketball. As a kid, he lived in Montana and North Dakota, places where the closest NBA arenas are hundreds of miles away. During his high school days as a forward in Williston, North Dakota, Jackson and his teammates often had to drive for five or six hours to play a game. Their biggest goal back then was to help Williston win a state championship. They did it in 1963. That was a sign of things to come for the thoughtful coach who became the best to ever roam an NBA sideline.

Jackson played a dozen years in the NBA, most of them with the New York Knicks. He struggled with back problems during most of his career and was used mostly as a reserve. That gave him plenty of time to watch and learn from his coaches, especially Red Holzman of the Knicks.

Holzman figured out a way to get a team filled with talented players such as guards Walt Frazier and Earl Monroe to play as a group while leading New York to NBA titles in 1970 and 1973. Holzman could tell that Jackson had all the ingredients needed to become a coach.

"He used to tell me, 'It's not rocket science, Phil. It's not rocket science,'" Jackson said. "He was pretty basic about his basketball:

see the ball on defense and hit the open man on offense. But he had a great feel for people and how to get them motivated."

It's a lesson that Jackson perfected in his own special way. While some coaches become a master at turning losing teams into winners, Jackson specialized in turning good teams into champions.

The Chicago Bulls had the best player in the world and another future All-Star when Jackson took over as head coach in 1990. Yet for all his talent, Michael Jordan hadn't been able to help the Bulls get past the Detroit Pistons in the playoffs. Jackson turned out to be the missing ingredient. Jackson taught his players the triangle offense. The triangle emphasized players, even great scorers like Jordan, sharing the ball.

At first, Jordan didn't want to run the triangle. But Jackson kept pushing it until Jordan bought in. With Jordan finally on board, the Bulls took off. Jackson guided the Bulls to six NBA championships in the 1990s.

Jackson moved on to the Los Angeles Lakers in 1999. Like Chicago, the Lakers had two superstars, center Shaquille O'Neal and guard Kobe Bryant, when Jackson arrived. Like Chicago, the Lakers kept coming up short in the playoffs. And just like he did in Chicago, Jackson helped his team figure it out. Jackson guided the Lakers to three straight championships between 2000 and 2002, tying Jackson with Red Auerbach for the most ever by an NBA coach.

Jackson took a brief break after the 2004 season, but a year later, he returned to the bench in

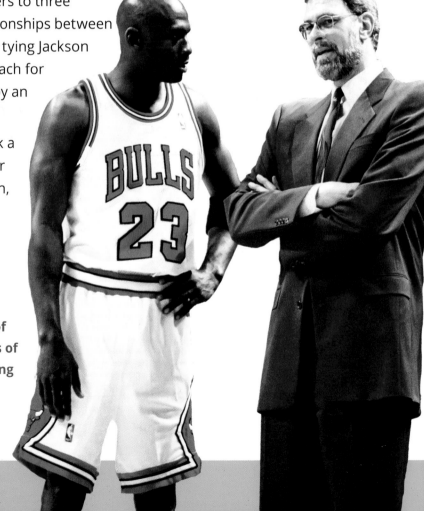

Phil Jackson coached some of the best players of all time, including Michael Jordan.

TEACHING PLAYERS

Jackson tried to teach his players lessons that extended far beyond the basketball court. He often bought books and placed them in their lockers. Some of the books were designed to help his players learn more about the game. Some of the books were about topics Jackson thought the players would find interesting.

Phil Jackson coached the Chicago Bulls to six championships.

Los Angeles, and the winning continued. Relying heavily on Bryant, the Lakers won back-to-back championships in 2009 and 2010, making the kid who grew up hundreds of miles from an NBA court the greatest NBA coach of all time.

HONORABLE MENTIONS

RED HOLZMAN: The other famous "Red" in NBA history, Holzman captured two titles with the New York Knicks in 1970 and 1973. Holzman was the 1970 NBA Coach of the Year and was inducted into the Hall of Fame as a coach in 1986. He finished his coaching career with 613 wins.

BILLY CUNNINGHAM: A five-time All-Star as a player, he won an NBA title with the Philadelphia 76ers in 1983. Cunningham finished with 454 wins in just eight seasons.

JERRY SLOAN: The longtime Utah Jazz coach won 1,127 games alongside Hall of Famers John Stockton and Karl Malone. He won a total of 1,221 games during his coaching tenures. Sloan never won a championship, but his Jazz reached the NBA Finals two straight years, losing to Michael Jordan and the Bulls both times.

GEORGE KARL: Karl's teams only missed the playoffs five times in 27 seasons. He took the Seattle SuperSonics to the 1996 NBA Finals. Karl coached six different teams and won 1,175 games. He was named NBA Coach of the Year in 2013, when he was with the Denver Nuggets.

BILL FITCH: Fitch guided Boston to a title in 1981 and earned a trip to the NBA Finals with Houston in 1986. In 25 seasons, he posted 944 wins and was named NBA Coach of the Year in 1976 and 1980.

K. C. JONES: After winning eight titles as a player with the Celtics in the 1960s, Jones won two more coaching the Celtics in 1984 and 1986. Jones won 552 games as a head coach in 11 seasons.

JACK RAMSAY: "Dr. Jack" led the Portland Trail Blazers to their only title in 1977. Ramsey won 864 games while coaching for the Philadelphia 76ers, Buffalo Braves, Portland Trail Blazers, and Indiana Pacers.

GLOSSARY

CENTER

Usually the tallest player on a basketball court, a center typically plays close to the basket on both offense and defense.

DRAFT

A system that allows teams to select players coming into a league.

DYNASTY

A team that has an extended period of success, usually winning multiple championships in the process.

FORWARD

A bigger player who is usually versatile and can both rebound and shoot.

GENERAL MANAGER

A team employee responsible for negotiating contracts with that team's players.

GUARD

Usually a smaller player who shoots from long range and is in charge of passing the ball to teammates.

ROOKIE

A professional athlete in his or her first year of competition.

MORE INFORMATION

ONLINE RESOURCES

To learn more about great NBA coaches, visit **abdobooklinks.com**. These links are routinely monitored and updated to provide the most current information available.

BOOKS

Ervin, Phil. *Total Basketball*. Minneapolis, MN: Abdo Publishing, 2017.

Graves, Will. *Make Me The Best Basketball Player*. Minneapolis, MN: Abdo Publishing, 2016.

Rivkin, Jennifer. *All Ball: Basketball's Greatest Players*. New York: Crabtree Publishing, 2015.

PLACE TO VISIT

NAISMITH MEMORIAL BASKETBALL HALL OF FAME
1000 Hall of Fame Avenue
Springfield, MA 01105
877–446–6752
hoophall.com

The Basketball Hall of Fame is like a museum dedicated to basketball. It highlights the greatest players, coaches, and moments in the sport's history. Many of the players and coaches mentioned in this book are enshrined there. It is home to more than 300 inductees and more than 40,000 square feet of basketball history.

INDEX

ABOUT THE AUTHOR

Will Graves has spent more than two decades as a sportswriter for several newspapers and the Associated Press, covering the NFL, MLB, the NHL, and the Olympics. He's also authored more than a dozen children's sports books. He lives in Pittsburgh, Pennsylvania, with his wife and their two children.